Jesus Is His Name

Rev. Daren Drzymala

Dedication

This book is dedicated to my parents Edward and Shirley Drzymala.

Table of Contents

Introduction

There are many religions in the world today with many claiming to be the true and only way, but there is one that stands alone and it is Christianity. What makes Christianity unlike any other religion is the person of Jesus Christ. When one mentions the name of Jesus Christ, feathers begin to ruffle and people even get upset. There is something about that name and the person of Jesus Christ that really bothers people. I have always said if you want to get ahead in the buffet line shout the name Jesus and people will get out of your way.

The person of Jesus Christ has literally affected over two-billion people worldwide; that says a lot about a man who only had a three year ministry. In this book I want to look at this person we call Jesus Christ, the founder of what is known as Christianity.

All over the world we hear about people converting to Christianity or giving their lives to Jesus Christ, and becoming Born Again Christians. What is this all about? Who is this man called Jesus, and what is his message. There are people in society who still doubt the existence of Christ, yet there is much historical evidence that points to the life, and death of Christ. Many Christian sources are very reliable when it comes to the life of Christ, including the Gospels, which are historically accurate. There are also many non-Christian writings as early as the life of Christ that talk about this man called Jesus. Even in Jewish writings we see Jesus mentioned in the Talmud, which is basically a commentary on the Old Testament, and many other traditions in Jewish writings that talk about the person of Jesus. Though not favorable, they still mention him.

There is much debate in religious circles about the role Jesus plays, but in Bible-centered Christianity there is a clear message of hope for a lost and dying world. In this book I would like to look at, focus on, present and preach this one named Jesus who is the Christ. I want you to read this book and have a better Biblical understanding of who Jesus is and what he is all about. Today people just talk about God and knowing God, or talk about a higher power in one's life. I want to get back to what it is all about, Jesus Christ.

People say that they have religion, well I agree with that, but I tell people I have a relationship with Jesus. Religion is man trying to reach up to God; Christianity is God reaching down to me in the person of Jesus Christ. So as you read this book ask yourself: "What do I know about Jesus? What do I believe about Jesus? Do I have a personal relationship with this one called Jesus Christ?"

Now let us look at a brief overview of what we will examine in this book:

Chapter One is called, "Jesus as seen in the Old Testament." Here we will look at many scriptures that show Jesus in the Old Testament, and how the scripture applies to Jesus Christ. Many people believe Jesus was a mythological person or just a New Testament person, but as we look at the first chapter we will see that Jesus is pictured all through the Old Testament. Numerous messianic prophecies point to Jesus as well, but consider Isaiah 9:6: *For unto us a child is born, unto us a son is given: and the government shall be upon his shoulder: and his name shall be called Wonderful, Counselor, the mighty God, the everlasting Father, The Prince of Peace.* This scripture clearly is a prophecy of the LORD Jesus Christ. Also in Isaiah 53 we see a clear description of the crucified Christ. The same goes for Psalm 22, which describes Christ on the cross. Psalm 16:10 proclaims the resurrection of Jesus: *For thou wilt not leave my soul in hell: neither wilt thou suffer thine Holy One to see corruption.* So there are many verses in the Old Testament that point to Jesus Christ, which we will examine in this first chapter.

Chapter Two is about the name of Jesus Christ. There is no more important name than the name Jesus Christ. Have you ever been given a nickname? When I was in high school my baseball coach called me "Dizzy Dean." At first I wondered why he called me Dizzy. Was there something about me that I did not know? I came to realize it was the name of a famous baseball player, and because I played baseball he gave me that nickname. Was there ever a time that you were called a name that was not so nice? I have been called many names in my ministry, some of which were not nice. There is no other name in history that stands out like the name of the LORD Jesus Christ. Today, many people use the name of Jesus as a curse word instead of for worship. The Bible is clear that God will not "hold him guiltless who taketh His name in vain." The Bible is clear that at the name of Jesus every knee will bow and tongue confess that Jesus is LORD. So for those who keep cussing the name of Jesus remember, one day you will fall on your face and call him Jesus, King of Kings and Lord of Lords. People, like the atheists who try to get God and Jesus out of everything, will one day bow their knee and worship Christ, however it will be too late and they will be cast into the lake of fire for all eternity.

Chapter Three is about Jesus and his ministry. Here we will discover that Jesus did not start his ministry until he was thirty years old and that it only lasted three years. Consider the billions of lives that have been changed by this Jesus over the years, and he only had a three year ministry, amazing! As one preacher put it, Jesus is either LORD or liar, which is it? When we examine the ministry of Jesus we will see that his ministry begins with prayer and how we should pray when we seek the LORD. His ministry also includes:

- Ministry to the sick. Many people in today's society are sick and need the great physician Jesus Christ.
- Ministry to the lost. As I said earlier, many people in society today are religious but still lost and are in need of a savior.
- Ministry to children is very important, however many churches today neglect outreach to children.
- Ministry to the sinful. There are many people who think the church is just for the righteous, but the Bible says it is a place for sinners.
- The ministry that Jesus had with a dead person. We will look at that later in detail.
- The ministry of compassion. There are many hurting people today, and many times Christians are killing their own. We need a ministry of compassion.
- The ministry to people who were possessed with demons. There are many accounts in scripture of people who had demons in them. I believe today we still see that.
- The ministry to doubters. There were many skeptics and doubters of Jesus back then and still are today. Jesus showed them his love and compassion.
- Then we see a message of warning to the religious leaders. Many people believe that the problem with America is the political system. I personally disagree with that view. I believe that the problem with America

today is its religious leaders and what they preach about Jesus.

Chapter Four is about the deity of Jesus Christ. One of the many major marks of a modern cult or a false religion is its view on Jesus Christ. Many religious cults preach that Jesus was a good man or that he was a prophet, but then deny that he was one-hundred percent God and one-hundred percent man. Jesus Christ is God himself, and we will look at verses to back this up.

Chapter Five is where we will look at how Jesus reacted to temptation. Most of us, if we are honest with ourselves, battle some type of spiritual temptation. We will see how Jesus responded to temptation.

Chapter Six will examine the promises of Christ. I am so glad that my savior has made many promises to me. The good news is that he keeps them.

Have you ever had someone promise something to you and later break that promise? Do you remember how you felt? Well Jesus is a promise keeper and will never let you down, no matter what comes your way.

Chapter Seven will examine Jesus and his descriptive return. I am so glad that Jesus is not going to leave me here on this old sinful earth, but one day will come back and call me home for all eternity.

Oh what a day that will be when my Jesus I shall see, when I look upon his face, the one who saved me by his grace. That will be awesome when that happens and for those who really want to know, I believe that Jesus' return is very, very near.

Chapter Eight will show Jesus revealed in the book of Revelation. The Revelation of Jesus Christ and end-time prophecy clearly portrays the person of Jesus Christ. We will look at it in greater detail.

Chapter Nine will look at Jesus and his gospel — what the gospel really is, and how it relates to mankind. There are many false gospels today that contain a false message and bring no hope to the lost. Unlike the gospel of Jesus Christ, which is a true message and a gospel of Hope.

Chapter Ten will examine the greatest invitation in the world, a personal invitation to all. I pray that when you read it, if you have never accepted this invitation you will do so.

That is a brief outline of what we will cover in this book. My prayer is that you will come away with a better understanding of who Jesus Christ is and what he is all about. Most importantly, I pray that when you read this book you will know for sure that you have a personal relationship with Jesus Christ. I pray that this book is a real blessing to you and all who read it.

Chapter One:
Jesus As Seen in the Old Testament

In this chapter we will look at many passages of scripture that point to Jesus Christ in the Old Testament. I am so glad that my savior is seen throughout the whole bible, not just in the New Testament. There are also many scriptures, called *theophanies*, which show a pre-Bethlehem appearance of Christ. Many times in the Old Testament you will see reference to the Angel of the LORD, which is another way of revealing Jesus in the Old Testament. Three men were thrown in the fire in Daniel chapter three, but four came out, one like the Son of God. This is a clear picture of Jesus Christ in the Old Testament.

Jesus – Creator of All

Scripture states in Genesis 1:26a: *And God said, let us make man in our image, after our likeness.* In this verse we see the word "our" for God, which reveals the trinity in creation, and we know that

Jesus is part of the triune God. If there was no trinity involved in creation, scripture would then state that God would make man in his own image, but the scriptures clearly state the word "our." Jesus clearly existed at the moment of creation.

Colossians 1:16 says, *For by him were all things created, that are in heaven, and that are in earth, visible and invisible, whether they be thrones, or dominions, or principalities, or powers: all things were created by him, and for him.* This passage in the New Testament is about none other than Jesus Christ in creation. Notice this verse states that Jesus created things in heaven. The streets of gold, the mansions of glory, the pearly gates, the wall of jasper, and the sea of glass as described in the book of Revelation.

Jesus – Victorious Over Sin

Jesus also created the grass, the seas, the animals and all other things on earth. Visible and invisible, things that cannot be seen were created by Christ, such as wind, angels and even demons, which are fallen angels. Christ also created Lucifer, a mighty angel who led worship in heaven. It was he, Lucifer, who then led a rebellion of angels:

> *For thou hast said in thine heart, I will ascend into heaven, I will exalt my throne above the stars of God: I will sit also upon the mount of the congregation, in the sides of the north. I*

will ascend above the heights of the clouds: I will be like the most High.
(Isaiah 14:13-14)

Lucifer's arrogance resulted in his fall from heaven and then being cast into hell. One-third of God's angels followed Lucifer and his rebellion, the result was eternity in the pit. Therefore, we see that all thrones and dominions were created by Christ as well as all principalities and powers, which are the different structures of Satan's army. Now we know that Jesus existed before time as we know it and was involved in the creation stage.

Genesis 3:15 declares: *And I will put enmity between thee and the woman, and between thy seed and her seed: it shall bruise thy head, and thou shalt bruise his heel.* This passage is known as the first gospel or evangelistic prophecy in which we are told that Satan will be defeated by the LORD Jesus Christ. Satan will bruise the heel of Christ as he is crucified, but Christ will bruise and crush the serpent's head. Here we see that Satan will do everything in his power to defeat Jesus, and ruin the hope for a lost and dying world. Nevertheless, Jesus will have the last word; He will win. Satan believes that the death of Christ on the cross is his victory, but unknown to him that the LORD Jesus will rise again and defeat Satan and all his angels. What a mighty picture of Christ in the Old Testament, The victory of the cross of Jesus Christ.

Genesis 3:20-21 states: *And Adam called his wife's name Eve; because she was the mother of all living. Unto Adam also and to his wife did the LORD God make coats of skins, and clothed them.* After Adam and Eve sinned in the garden they saw their nakedness and felt their separation from God. God gave Adam and Eve coats to cover themselves that were made from the skin of innocent animals whose blood was shed so they could be covered.

Do you see it? Here is a perfect picture of the blood of the LORD Jesus Christ that was shed on Calvary's mountain to not only cover our sins but to wash them away. In the Old Testament when a sacrifice for sin was made it was for atonement for sin, or a covering, the washing comes later. Let's look at it this way; say I were to show you a garbage can full of garbage, then I put the lid on it. You would not see the garbage but it would still be there. That is what atonement did for the saints in the Old Testament. They had their sins covered from the judgment of God.

Abraham and Isaac

Genesis 22:13 declares: *And Abraham lifted up his eyes, and looked and behold behind him a ram caught in a thicket by his horns: and Abraham went and took the ram, and offered him up for a burnt offering in the stead of his son.* Earlier in Genesis 22:2 God told Abraham to take his son Isaac and offer him as a sacrifice to the LORD. Abraham was a dedicated man of God and was willing to do whatever God asked him to do, so he took his son to the land of Moriah to offer him as a sacrifice. When Isaac asked where the lamb for the sacrifice was, I am sure that he had begun to wonder what was up and may even wondered if his dad was going to kill him. This had to tear at the heart of Abraham as he saw the pondering and hurt of his son.

Abraham made a profound statement in Genesis 22:8: *And Abraham said, my son, God will provide himself a lamb for a burnt offering: so they went both of them together*. Notice that Abraham said *God will provide himself a lamb*. God made a way for a substitute sacrifice to be made so that Isaac did not have to be offered.

Jesus is the substitute for you and me. Because of our sin, you and I deserve death. Apostle Paul wrote in Romans 6:23a, *For the wages of sin is death*. The result of mankind's sin is physical and spiritual death. We all deserve to die and go to hell, but God took our place on Calvary's mountain and is our substitute sacrifice. I am so thankful for Jesus and what he did on the cross for you and for me, another perfect picture of Jesus Christ.

Moses – Deliverer of Israel

Let us now look at Moses as the deliverer for the Israelites in Exodus 3. God told Moses that he would use him to bring the Israelites out of bondage from Egypt. Imagine the amazing feeling Moses must have had, and how nervous he must have been to think that he would lead God's people to freedom? Now picture this deliverance ministry of Moses and how it unfolded. Moses tried to make excuses why he could not lead so God said that his brother Aaron would be his spokesman. Moses and Aaron went to Pharaoh and said that God told them to let his people go. Of course Pharaoh did no such thing, so God, through Moses and Aaron, did signs to get Pharaoh's attention, even using different plagues to convince the Egyptian ruler to let the Israelites go:

Water became blood. Can you imagine that wherever the Egyptians went to drink the water was pure blood? They were unable to bathe, cook, drink or do anything with water because it was blood. Nevertheless, Pharaoh would not let God's people go so God sent another plague.

1. The plague of frogs. The land was infested with frogs; everywhere they went there were frogs. In their house, in their beds, in their living rooms were frogs galore. Yet Pharaoh would not let them go.

2. The plague of lice. God had Aaron stretch out his hand with his rod and strike the ground so that the dust became lice that infested the entire land. Still Pharaoh resisted God.

3. The plague of flies. That would drive me crazy! I would tell the Israelites to get out, but Pharaoh did not.

4. The plague of death for cattle, horses, asses and camels. Pharaoh's heart did not soften to let God's people go.

5. The plague of boils upon man and beast. Throughout all the land everyone had ugly blistering boils on their bodies. I would be screaming to Pharaoh to get rid of the Israelites, they are

causing us too many problems, just let them go so we can live in peace, but Pharaoh would not do it.

6. The plague of hail mingled with fire. The Egyptians were not only being hit with large hail stones but with fire as well. They were being burned and even killed because of it. What a picture for those who reject Jesus as deliverer, they will face fire in hell for all eternity. Still Pharaoh would not let God's people go.

7. The plague of locusts or grasshoppers throughout all the land. No matter where they went, there they were. Scripture states that they filled the houses. Again I hear the Egyptians crying let them go! But Pharaoh hardened his heart, and did not budge.

8. The plague of darkness throughout the land. The people could not see anyone or anything, but still Pharaoh would not allow God's people go.

9. The plague of death of the firstborn. Pharaoh finally let the people go after this plague claimed his firstborn son.

10. How do we see a picture of Christ in these plagues? Moses was the man God chose to bring deliverance to the Israelites. Jesus is whom God used to bring deliverance to all of mankind, setting us free from the bondage of sin and death. If the Son sets you free you shall be free indeed.

Jesus – King of Israel and of the Jews

Let us look at Numbers 24:17: *I shall see him, but not now: I shall behold him but not nigh: there shall come a star out of Jacob, and a Sceptre shall rise out of Israel.* In this passage we see Jesus as the king of Israel and of the Jews. In Jesus day, the Jews thought that messiah's kingdom would come and set them free from the Romans. However, the kingdom that Jesus preached was not of this world, but was of a heavenly world. The people who yelled "Hosanna to the LORD" also yelled "Crucify him!" when they realized that he was not going to bring his kingdom on earth. The Jews were upset when the sign "King of the Jews" was placed on the cross above Jesus' head, but the title was true whether they believed it or not. Here in Numbers we see Jesus the true king of the Jews, and soon to be coming the great King of Kings and LORD of LORDS.

The Tabernacle of Moses included a candlestick of pure gold (Exodus 25:31-40) that symbolized the light of the world, and Jesus is a perfect picture of light to a lost and dark world. Just how dark is our society that it needs the light of Jesus? Think about it; we live in a world where people hate one another for the color of their skin, people kill each other, engage in sexual sin, molest children, and so on. This is a dark, dark world in desperate need of light. Jesus said that he was the light of the world (John 8:12).

If you are a Christian you are to shine the light of Jesus so that people will see your savior and give their hearts to him. The Bible says to *let our lights so shine before men that they may see your good works and glorify your Father who is in heaven* (Matthew 5:16). An old children's song said, "hide it under a bushel no, I'm gonna let it shine, and won't let Satan blow it out."

Let the light that shined in the tabernacle as a picture of Jesus Christ, shine all over the world and through your testimony.

While in the wilderness, Israel complained to Moses and Aaron about there being no water, so God told Moses to take the rod and strike the rock and then water would come out (Numbers 20:1-10). Jesus is the rock that gives us living water so that we will never thirst again. What a perfect picture of Christ as the Rock. We can also learn to build our churches on the Rock of Jesus, and they will stand the test of time. Our families need to stand on the Rock so that when the storms of adversity come, we will stand firm on Jesus Christ. We must build our lives on the Rock of Jesus so that we can withstand whatever comes our way.

May you put the Rock of Ages under your feet today, and stand when Satan's armies come against you.

Jesus – The Bread from Heaven

And the children of Israel did eat manna fourty years until they came to a land inhabited; they did eat manna, until they came to the borders of the land of Canaan (Exodus 16:35). Here we see that Israel wandered in the wilderness for forty years. It would be difficult to imagine being in the wilderness for four days, let alone forty years. Throughout those years they complained constantly, sounds like the church today, always complaining. Let us be a people of praise not pity.

The picture of Israel eating manna is a perfect picture of Jesus being our bread from heaven. *And Jesus said unto them, I am the bread of life: he that cometh to me shall never hunger* (John 6:35). You can see clearly here that Jesus is the bread of life and that he truly brings satisfaction to your life. You may remember being young and early in the morning smelled the bread your mother was baking, how it tasted and satisfied, but eventually you were hungry again. With the bread of life you will always be satisfied and never hungry again.

Last I would like to discuss a very important passage about Christ in the Old Testament. We have already talked about Jesus being a picture of a deliverer as seen in the life of Moses. In preparation for the ninth plague the Israelites were told to put lamb's blood on the top of their doorposts from top to bottom and from side to side. When the death angel came and saw the blood he passed over, but where he did not see the blood the firstborn were killed. The death angel passed over the Egyptian homes and found no blood so the firstborn were killed. Wailing and weeping was heard among the Egyptians because of the death of their children, but when the angel saw blood over the doorposts of Israel he passed by. What a perfect picture of the LORD Jesus Christ! When he sees his blood on our hearts, he passes by. The picture of the cross is seen because the blood was posted top to bottom and side to side. Thank God for the cross of Jesus, without it there would be no hope.

As you can see, the Jesus whom we preach and talk about is seen throughout all the scriptures. He is alive and well today in the hearts of those who trust him as their savior.

Chapter Two:

Jesus and His Marvelous Name

There is a song I love to sing... "Jesus, Jesus, Jesus, sweetest name I know fills my every longings keeps me singing as I go." I love to sing this song because it talks about the most precious name to me, the name of Jesus. I would like to look at several names of Jesus in the scriptures and how they are applied to our lives.

Jesus – Savior

The Bible says in Matthew 1:21: *And she shall bring forth a son, and thou shalt call his name JESUS: for he shall save his people from their sins*. The name Jesus means, "Savior." This is an awesome name because it indicates that one not only needs to be saved, but can be saved. The Bible declares in Romans 3:23 that all mankind are sinners and that because of sin we deserve death in hell as our punishment.

Let us take a moment to ponder the punishment for sin and what happens to lost souls without a Savior. Some people believe that once you die that is it, but that is not what the scriptures teach. The Bible talks about a place called hell and Jesus preached more about it then anyone in the scriptures.

The Bible describes this eternal punishment as weeping and gnashing of teeth (Matthew 25:30). Matthew 22:13 calls it a place of outer darkness, while Luke 16:23 it calls it a place of torment; Mark 9:44 says the fire there is not quenched. This shows me that it is real fire that torments people forever, it cannot be quenched and it never ends. Just like people have eternal life in heaven there is also eternal life in hell. Revelation 9:2 says hell is a bottomless pit, Revelation 14:11 calls it a place of no rest.

Hell is not a place most people would want to go, but millions of souls are dropping into a Christ-less eternity every second. We need a savior to rescue the perishing people from this burning hell. The late Dr. B.R. Lakin preached a message on the "Blissful heaven or the burning hell - the choice is yours."

When I consider a savior I must look at three parts of salvation: I am saved, I am being saved and I shall be saved. Now please stay with me—I know I am saved without a doubt. I am presently saved from the penalty of sin, which is hell. I am daily saved from the power of sin, which is sanctification. One day when I am with my LORD and savior Jesus Christ, I will be saved from the presence of sin. Therefore, the name Jesus, which means "savior," is so important and truly applies to the believer in Jesus Christ.

Jesus – Redeemer

The next name is found in Galatians 3:13: *Christ hath redeemed us from the curse of the law, being made a curse for us: for it is written, Cursed is everyone that hangeth on a tree.* The Bible declares Jesus as redeemer of mankind. A redeemer is one who buys something or someone back. Jesus redeemed us, or bought us back from the slave market of sin and death which is controlled by Satan himself. You and I were in prison chains before we trusted Jesus as Savior, and when we accepted him, he set us free and bought us back.

Another song I like to sing is "Redeemed." It says, "Redeemed how I love to proclaim it, redeemed by the blood of the lamb."

Do you love to proclaim it and tell people about it? Are you excited about what Jesus did for you?

Mark 16:15 says to preach the gospel to everyone. This is not a calling, but a command. Though I am commanded to tell people about Jesus and how he redeemed me, I want to; it is my burning desire.

Is sharing about Jesus your desire as well? Remember, you have the answer for cancer, not of the body, but of the soul, and you should shout it from the mountain tops about Jesus as redeemer.

Jesus – Holy One

But ye denied the Holy One, and the just, and desired a murderer to be granted unto you (Acts 3:14). Jesus is called the Holy One, which is important

29

because if Jesus was not holy he could not pay for the sins of the world. He is perfect in all manner of speech, works and actions, and he has never sinned. Not only does that show us that he was the unblemished sacrifice for sins, but it teaches us also how to live.

As obedient children, not fashioning yourselves according to the former lusts in your ignorance; But as he which hath called you is holy, so be ye holy in all manner of conversation; Because it is written, Be ye holy; for I am holy (1 Peter 3:14-16). Here we see a call for Christians to be holy in the sight of God. Some Christians believe they can come to a point of being sinless, but I do not. I believe that we can sin less, but not be sinless.

The church of God has a great need for old fashioned holiness and separation from the worldly standards that have infected the culture. There are many devices that Christians get caught up in that I believe we ought to stay away from such as: drinking, swearing, smoking, watching dirty programs, or programs that mock Jesus Christ. We need, as much as possible, to be more like the Master of theology, Jesus. Scripture says we shall be like Him when we see Him, but let us strive for holiness today. Then the world will see Jesus in us.

Jesus – Rose of Sharon

Therefore if any man be in Christ, he is a new creature: old things are passed away; behold, all things are become new (2 Corinthians 5:17). Jesus is the "Rose of Sharon" which means "giver of new life." When one accepts Jesus as Savior he becomes a new person, the old passes away. There should be a change in a truly repentant person who puts their faith and trust in Jesus Christ. We should not talk, walk, or act the same way, but should be transformed:

I Beseech you therefore, brethren, by the mercies of God, that ye present your bodies a living sacrifice, holy, acceptable unto God, which is your reasonable service. And be not conformed to this world: but be ye transformed by the renewing of your mind, that ye may prove what is that good, and acceptable, and perfect, will of God.
(Romans 12:1-2)

To live a different life is only reasonable considering what the LORD has done for you. The scripture talks about renewing your mind, otherwise garbage in and garbage out will happen in your life.

Jesus – Mediator

For there is one God, and one mediator between God and men, the man Christ Jesus (1 Timothy 2:5). If a person wants to go to God he does not need to go through a priest, a pastor or a deacon, but only through the LORD Jesus. People try to reach God in many ways but the only way is through Jesus. I strongly believe that when a person prays and seeks God, they need to pray in and through Jesus name.

Jesus – Bridegroom

Matthew 9:15 refers to Jesus as the "Bridegroom." *And Jesus said unto them, can the children of the bride chamber mourn, as long as the bridegroom is with them? But the days will come, when the bridegroom shall be taken from them, and then shall they fast.* The church of Jesus Christ is the bride of Christ. What a beautiful day that will be when we believers, as the Bride of Christ, enter our marriage relationship with Jesus. We will love Christ in an unending way and will sacrifice anything for him and even lay down our lives for the savior.

Are you willing as a Christian to be the partner you ought to be, to love the LORD with all your heart, soul and might? Remember Jesus will do anything for you in this relationship. Will you do the same?

Jesus – Chief Cornerstone

We see in Ephesians 2 that Jesus is the Chief Cornerstone:

Now therefore ye are no more strangers and foreigners, but fellow citizens with the saints, and of the household of God; And are built upon the foundation of the apostles and prophets, Jesus Christ himself being the chief cornerstone.
(Ephesians 2:19-20)

Christ is the main foundation for every person who is a believer. Can you imagine having a house built on a foundation of sand? The house would not be there very long, but would sink. This is what happens to a person who tries to build their life on any other foundation than Jesus Christ, it will sink and collapse.

Jesus – Head of the Church

That we henceforth be no more children, tossed to and fro, and carried bout with every wind of doctrine, by the sleight of men, and cunning craftiness, whereby they lie in wait to deceive; But speaking the truth in love, may grow up into him in all things, which is the head, even Christ: From whom the whole body fitly joined together and compacted by that which every joint supplieth, according to the effectual working in the measure of every part, maketh increase of the body unto the edifying of itself in love.
(Ephesians 4:14-16)

This passage reveals much about the Church and Christ being the head. First we see that we are not to be tossed to and fro by every wind of doctrine. Many preachers today are not "caught up in doctrine," but doctrine is essential to the Christian faith. What a person believes about God, the Bible, the Blood, Jesus and so on is very important. The word "doctrine" is used many times in scripture and basically means "teachings." I am one who is not ashamed to call myself a

Fundamental Baptist preacher who believes in sound biblical doctrine.

People are all over the map when it comes to theology and Bible teaching which can drive you crazy. Therefore, we must study to show ourselves approved and "rightly divide the word of truth."

We must "speak the truth in love." Too many Christians become harsh when proclaiming God's Word to the point where they do not share in love. We must love the sinner and hate the sin. Regarding the issue of homosexuality, we are to love the people but hate the sin so we can show them the life-changing power of Jesus Christ.

We must remember that the whole body is fitly joined together. There are millions of believers but one body and one head, the LORD Jesus Christ. Let us work together without compromising our theology, to win as many people as possible to Jesus Christ.

Jesus – Author of Eternal Salvation

And being made perfect, he became the author of eternal salvation unto all them that obey him (Hebrews 5:9). Jesus is the author and finisher of our eternal salvation. Salvation comes only through the LORD Jesus Christ, who was, and is, and is to come.

Jesus – the Resurrection and the Life

Jesus said unto her, I am the resurrection, and the life: he that believeth in me, though he were

34

dead, yet shall he live: And whosoever liveth and believeth in me shall never die. Believest thou this.
(John 11:25-26)

Jesus promised that we will rise again someday all because Jesus himself came back to life. Therefore, if someone tells you this life is all there is, that you live and then die and that is it, point him to this passage of scripture.

Jesus – King of Peace

To whom also Abraham gave a tenth part of all; first being by interpretation King of righteousness, and after that also King of Salem, which is King of peace (Hebrews 7:2). This is in reference to Jesus, the Prince of Peace. Today everywhere you go people are looking for peace but finding none. The only way to have peace is to come to the King of Peace which is Jesus Christ.

Jesus – Truth

Jesus saith unto him, I am the way, the truth, and the life: no man cometh unto the father, but by me (John 14:6). This passage calls Jesus the truth. *Ye shall know the truth, and the truth shall make you free* (John 8:32). The Bible also declares: *...thy word is truth* (John 17:17). God's Word is pure truth, as mentioned in Psalm 12:6-7. There are no errors in the Word of God; it is kept by God's preserving power. The Word of God talks about science, geography, history and so on, yet unlike any other book it stands the test of time. The Bible says to preach the Word, not opinions or philosophy.

Jesus – The Christ

Then charged he his disciples that they should tell no man that he was Jesus the Christ (Matthew 16:20). Jesus is the Christ, the anointed one or messiah. Jesus is the messiah that the people rejected, and he came to give life to all who believe.

As you can see in this chapter the name of Jesus is marvelous and worthy of praise. Revelation 4:11 reveals the saints and angels proclaiming: *Thou art worthy, O Lord, to receive glory and honour and power: for thou hast created all things, and for thy pleasure they are and were created.* Revelation 4:8 declares: *And the four beasts had each of them six wings about him; and they were full of eyes within: and they rest not day and night, saying, Holy, holy, holy, Lord God Almighty, which was, and is, and is to come.* Here we see praise to the holiness of the triune God.

For those who like to deny the trinity, please also read about Jesus in 1 John 5:7: *For there are three that bear record in heaven, the Father, the Word, and the Holy Ghost: and these three are one.* There is no debating the triune Godhead of which Jesus Christ is part. Thanks be to God for Jesus Christ and His saving power.

Chapter Three:

Jesus and His Mighty Ministry

As we begin this chapter I would like to look at different areas of the ministry of Jesus Christ. As stated earlier, Jesus' ministry lasted just three years, but it was the most powerful and dynamic ministry ever. The person and work of Jesus in those three years changed the lives of people forever. Lives are still changing today through his eternal ministry and message.

My Father's Business

Before we begin, we will look at an amazing verse of scripture about Jesus' early life in Nazareth: *And the child grew, and waxed strong in spirit, filled with wisdom: and the grace of God was upon him* (Luke 2:40). I believe that his ministry began even then in many ways. This should help us understand that children today, if taught correctly from the scriptures, can grow up in the wisdom of the LORD.

Further on we read that Jesus and his earthly parents went to Jerusalem for the yearly feast of the Passover:

> *Now his parents went to Jerusalem every year at the feast of the passover. And when he was twelve years old, they went up to Jerusalem after the custom of the feast. And when they had fulfilled the days, as they returned, the child Jesus tarried behind in Jerusalem; and Joseph and his mother knew not of it. But they, supposing him to have been in the company, went a day's journey; and they sought him among their kinsfolk and acquaintance. And when they found him not, they turned back again to Jerusalem, seeking him. And it came to pass, that after three days they found him in the temple, sitting in the midst of the doctors, both hearing them, and asking them questions. And all that heard him were astonished at his understanding and answers. And when they saw him, they were amazed: and his mother said unto him, Son, why hast thou thus dealt with us? behold, thy father and I have sought thee sorrowing. And he said unto them, How is it that ye sought me? wist ye not that I must be about my Father's business?*
> Luke 2:41-49 (KJV)

As Jesus' parents returned to Nazareth they did not realize that Jesus was not with them. When they discovered his absence, they turned back to seek him and found him after three days. Can you imagine the feeling of his parents not being able to find their son? This must have been devastating to them. When Jesus was finally found, he was not playing with other kids, playing a trick on his parents or running away, he was in the Temple discussing theology with the leaders of the Law.

Jesus had to be some amazing child at twelve years old to be discussing the Law with religious leaders trained in the Word. When his parents saw him they basically said, why did you do this to us? The response of Jesus in verse 49 is very interesting: *And he said unto them, How is it that ye sought me? wist ye not that I must be about my father's business?*

Jesus gave a profound answer to his parents by saying that he was doing the work of God. What a statement from such a young boy! He knew that when he was talking to the doctors of the Law that he was doing the ministry he was called to by God.

Are you about the Father's business? Are you doing the work of the LORD? If not, start today and you will be blessed beyond measure.

The Importance of Prayer

As we examine the ministry of Jesus, we will focus on different areas of ministry in which the LORD could use us. It is very important first to see what Jesus did early every day. *And in the morning, rising up a great while before day, he went out and departed into a solitary place, and there prayed* (Mark 1:35). The ministry of Jesus was built on prayer which is why he was able to accomplish such effective works of God.

The scripture states that Jesus began his day talking to the Father. That is how we Christians need to start our day as well, seeking the LORD and his wisdom in all that we attempt to do for God. Do you pray? How often? King David stated every morning, noon, and night he sought the LORD. I encourage you to have a special prayer life with the LORD. There is power in prayer. Like I tell preachers, the power of the pulpit is the prayers of the pews.

Jesus not only started his ministry in prayer, he taught us how to pray. Look at Matthew 6:9-13:

> *After this manner therefore pray ye: Our Father which art in heaven, Hallowed be thy name. Thy kingdom come. Thy will be done in earth, as it is in heaven. Give us this day our daily bread. And forgive us our debts, as we forgive our debtors. And lead us not into temptation, but deliver us from evil: For thine is the kingdom, and the power, and the glory, for ever. Amen.*

This prayer was given to help us as believers learn how to pray, not to just repeat the same words every day (for the Bible warns about vain repetition). Let us look at this prayer and what we can glean from it.

Our Father indicates that when we pray we should have a personal relationship with God. Everyone, spiritually speaking, has a father.

Those who know Jesus Christ in a personal way can call God their Father. For those who do not know Christ in a personal way, the Bible states in John 8:44: *Ye are of your father the devil.* This is a very strong statement, but it is true. The devil is the spiritual father of unbelievers. This makes some harsh preaching, but we cannot compromise the truth of God's Word.

If you are an unbeliever, I encourage you to give your heart to Jesus today. If you are a believer then you can approach the throne of God boldly and seek your heavenly father.

Hallowed be thy name. Here we see praise and adoration to the LORD. So often when we pray all we do is ask for something. That is not what prayer is about; it is a time of worship between us and the LORD.

Give God praise and thanksgiving for all that he has done for you, for all his blessings, and even the trials he has allowed. Scripture says in everything give thanks, not just for the good, but for the not so good, even though this is hard to do.

Thy kingdom come, Thy will be done. When you pray make sure you pray in accordance with the will of God and not your will. It is vitally important to pray "God's will be done" in everything we pray about. The Bible also says that when you give thanks for everything, this is the will of God. Some things are hard to give thanks for but remember that God is sovereign and in complete control. Whatsoever he wills, he does.

One type of prayer that some believers pray that is worth mentioning is the "name it, claim it" prayer. This is a lie from hell! Believers need not tell God what he must give them, or believe if they say it, it shall come to pass. That is totally unscriptural. So when believers pray, do so in accordance with the will of God.

Give us this day our daily bread. We can now come and seek God for things that we need, not what we want. God is a provider to his children and he will not let the righteous be forsaken. We can seek the face of God for spiritual needs, physical needs, financial needs, and whatever we need. Remember God owns the cattle on a thousand hills, and can meet anyone's needs.

Forgive us our debts. We can seek forgiveness in the LORD whenever we need it. *If we confess our sins, he is faithful and just to forgive us our sins, and to cleanse us from all unrighteousness* (1 John 1:9). Jesus is faithful to forgive us no matter what sins we have done. Some people may think that they have done such horrible sins, that God will not forgive them, but that is just another lie from hell. The blood of Jesus cleanseth from ALL sin, no matter what it is or how bad it is. And remember, our sins are cast into the sea of God's forgetfulness to be remembered no more. As far as the east is from the west, they are removed! Thanks be to God for forgiveness.

...as we forgive our debtors. Too often we Christians hold grudges against other people and will not forgive. However, we must remember

that Christ has forgiven us, therefore how much more should we forgive others.

And lead us not into temptation, but deliver us from evil. We must pray to God to protect us from evil and the evil one. Satan is like a roaring lion seeking whom he may devour, so we must put on the whole armor of God as taught in Ephesians 6:10-17.

As you can see, prayer is powerful. Jesus not only prayed, but gave us a good example of how to pray.

Jesus' Ministry of Healing

And Jesus departed from thence and came nigh unto the sea of Galilee; and went up into a mountain, and sat down there. And great multitudes came unto him, having with them those that were lame, blind, dumb, maimed, and many others, and cast them down at Jesus feet; and he healed them: Insomuch that the multitude wondered, when they saw the dumb to speak, the maimed to be whole, the lame to walk, and the blind to see: and they glorified the God of Israel.
(Matthew 15:29-31)

Jesus' ministry included those people who had physical problems. Great multitudes of people from all over came to Jesus because many of them heard about the great works he did. The blind were touched by

Jesus and made whole. Others could not hear so Jesus touched them so they could hear sound for the first time in their lives. Yet others had never walked and Jesus healed them. How awesome that must have been.

Let us enter into a little theological discussion here. I totally believe in the healing power of God and that he can touch anyone at any time as he sees fit. Where I differ is when some man claims to have the gift of healing, yet cannot heal everyone like Jesus did. Many of these so-called "faith healers" set up meetings and claim to heal, but does not go to veteran's or children's hospitals to heal. Let me say this, I believe the gift of healing was an early apostolic gift for a sign to unbelieving Israel and is not in operation today. Nevertheless, the God of healing is still on the throne and can heal as he wills. The ultimate healing is when a believer goes to be with the LORD in heaven.

Jesus' Ministry to the Dead

Jesus also had a ministry to dead people. Now let me clarify something: I do not believe in the raising of the dead today; *...it is appointed unto man once to die, but after this the judgment* (Hebrews 9:27). That all said, Jesus in His earthly ministry did raise people from the dead.

Mary, Martha and Lazarus were friends of Jesus who lived in Bethany. According to John chapter 11, Lazarus was sick so his sisters sent for Jesus to come heal him. They knew of the power that Jesus had and the great wonders he had done. When Jesus finally came the sisters were upset because Lazarus died and had been in the grave for four days.

When Jesus arrived he told Mary and Martha that Lazarus would rise again. The sisters thought Jesus meant in the last day, which was well known in Jewish thought.

> *And when he thus had spoken, he cried with a loud voice, Lazarus, come forth. And he that was dead came forth, bound hand and foot with graveclothes: and his face was bound about with a napkin. Jesus saith unto them, Loose him, and let him go.*
> (John 11:43-44)

Here Jesus literally raised a man back to life who had been dead for four days. Notice that Jesus called Lazarus by name. Could you imagine if he just said, "Come forth"? All of the graves would have opened and there would have been mass chaos because all of the dead would have been raised.

For me, one of the greatest ministries is the funeral of a believer. The saint is in heaven, which makes this is an awesome opportunity to minister to people and share the gospel of Jesus Christ.

Jesus' Ministry to Children

> *Then were there brought unto him little children, that he should put his hands on them, and pray: and the disciples rebuked them.*

But Jesus said, Suffer little children, and forbid them not, to come unto me: for of such is the kingdom of heaven.
(Matthew 19:13-14)

One of the most important ministries a church or individual can have is ministry to young impressionable children. This passage shows that people brought their children to Jesus to pray for them and with them. Some of the disciples, however, acted like many people do today, that children are a bother. Nevertheless, Jesus made it very clear that they were to let them come to him!

I love the lyrics, "Jesus loves the little children, all the children of the world, red and yellow, black and white, they are precious in his sight." Other passages in scripture warn of offending a little child, saying it would be better to have a millstone hung around your neck and to be cast into the sea (Matthew 18:6). I am staunchly pro-life, and believe that abortion is an abomination in front of a Holy God. I am not pro-life because of my political affiliation, but because the Bible preaches it. Furthermore, Jesus Christ himself is pro-life. I say to declare the love of God to little children and suffer them to come unto the LORD.

Jesus' Ministry of Compassion

In those days the multitude being very great, and having nothing to eat, Jesus called his disciples unto him, and saith unto them, I

have compassion on the multitude, because
they have now been with me three days, and
have nothing to eat…
(Mark 8:1-2)

This passage reveals Jesus' compassion for more than four-thousand hungry people. Have you ever been hungry? If so, then you will probably agree that it is not a good feeling. These people had been without food for three days. Jesus could have said it was their fault and they should have packed a lunch, but that is not how he responded. Jesus was moved with compassion.

We as Christians need to show compassion toward those who are sick, hurting, have emotional problems, are homeless or whatever has come into their lives. If we just say "God help you" and then go on our way, we have missed the mark. Jesus had a lot on his mind but he still loved the people with compassion. Our churches need to show the love and compassion of Jesus to a lost and dying world, then we will truly make a difference in people's lives.

Jesus' Mastery over Creation

Now it came to pass on a certain day, that
he went into a ship with his disciples: and he
said unto them, Let us go over unto the other
side of the lake. And they launched forth. But
as they sailed he fell asleep: and there came
down a storm of wind on the lake; and they
were filled with water, and were in jeopardy.

*And they came to him, and awoke him, saying,
master, master, we perish. Then he arose, and
rebuked the wind and the raging of the water:
and they ceased, and there was a calm. And
he said unto them, Where is your faith? And
they being afraid wondered, saying one to
another, What manner of man is this! for he
commandeth even the winds and water, and
they obey him.*
(Luke 8:22-25)

Jesus even controlled nature. Put yourself on
this ship. A wicked storm hits and the winds and the
waves become violent to the point where you think
that you might even drown. Yet while the storm was
going on, the LORD Jesus was asleep.

I know myself that when a thunderstorm happens, I
cannot sleep. Being on a ship during a major storm like
the disciples were, I for sure would be unable to sleep.

Jesus, however, had the peace of God upon him
and knew that he controlled the storm. When he
arose, he calmed the winds and waters. The disciples
were amazed that even nature obeyed his voice. The
character of the omnipotence of God is demonstrated
here, for no one could command nature as Jesus did.

There is also another point to this story. Maybe
you are going through a major trial in your life and
are in the midst of a storm that is raging wild. There
is a person named Jesus who can calm your storm by
saying, "Peace be still, all is well." You will always
have trials and tribulations, but Jesus will help you
through anything; just trust him.

Jesus' Ministry to Sinners

John chapter 4 relates Jesus' ministry to a sinful Samaritan woman. He went to her for water, which surprised her because Jews did not interact with Samaritans. Jesus then told her that he could give her water so that she would never thirst again. He also said that this water would spring up into everlasting life. The woman wanted this water so she would thirst no more.

The Samaritan woman had a spiritual void in her life. She knew something was missing and she wanted it. Jesus told her to go call her husband to which she responded, "I have no husband." Jesus knew this about her and then told her that she had had five husbands and the man she was with now was not her husband. Later she realized that Jesus was the messiah promised for the Jews.

Jesus could have really brought this woman down and condemned her, but ministry to sinful people is why he came. Like Jesus, we need to have a ministry to reach sinful people. Who needs a physician, the sick or the healthy? We can show them the love and forgiveness of God through Jesus Christ.

Jesus' Authority over the Demonic World

Jesus revealed His authority over the demonic world in Mark chapter 5 in the account of the demon-possessed man of Gadara. Verse 8 declares, *For he said unto him, come out of the man, thou unclean spirit.*

Have you ever heard someone say that if they could get their hands on Satan they would take care of him? We do not wrestle against flesh and blood, and Satan is not omnipresent, so we battle demons instead. Many people in this world are demon possessed and the only way for them to gain victory is through the power of the LORD Jesus Christ.

Let us consider this theologically. Christians cannot be possessed by demons, but they can be oppressed by demons. There are deliverance ministries that "call demons out" of Christians, but this cannot be true. The Bible teaches that our bodies are the temple of the Holy Spirit and what fellowship hath light with darkness. The Holy Spirit indwells believers at the moment of salvation so Satan and his demons are not welcome.

Jesus' Ministry to Doubters

Afterward he appeared unto the eleven as they sat at meat, and unbraided them with their unbelief and hardness of heart, because they believed not them which had seen him after he was risen.
(Mark 16:14)

This is a ministry to doubters. Jesus' own disciples did not believe in his resurrection until he sat and ate with them. Likewise, there are many doubters today known as atheists, agnostics, and humanists. These doubters need to be shown the truth through God's Word. Other means to reach them include apologetics, which contends for the faith using history, science, archeology, and other types of evidence.

What amazes me is how the disciples who doubted after Jesus' death became fundamentalist preachers after an encounter with the risen Christ. When a person truly meets Jesus things change. Look at the life of Saul. He was a Pharisee of Pharisees who persecuted the church. Then he met the LORD on the Damascus Road and became a powerful missionary preacher for the church. Amazing things happen when skeptics trust the risen Christ.

Jesus' Ministry to the Lost

For the Son of man is come to save that which is lost (Matthew 18:11). The primary ministry of Christ is to reach the lost and to help men and women become reconciled to God. Are you talking to people and witnessing about the Savior? A great ministry is old-fashioned soul winning. Proverbs 11:30 says: *He that winneth souls is wise*. Now go out and win the lost for Jesus.

Chapter Four:

Jesus and His Divine Deity

Many of the cults today deny the very deity of the LORD Jesus Christ, which is a fundamental doctrine of the Christian faith. A person who denies this doctrine cannot be a true Christian.

This chapter will examine ten scriptures that support teaching the deity of Jesus Christ. However, we must first ask what the deity of Christ is. This is the doctrine that Jesus is one-hundred percent God and one-hundred percent man. Though this may be hard to comprehend it is indeed a biblical doctrine of major importance.

Jesus – the Word of God

In the beginning was the Word, and the Word was with God, and the Word was God. The same was in the beginning with God. All things were made by him; and without him was not any thing made that was made.
(John 1:1-3)

*And the Word was made flesh, and dwelt
among us, (and we beheld his glory, the glory
as of the only begotton of the Father,) full of
grace and truth.*
(John 1:14)

These passages reveal a few things about Jesus.
We see that he is called the Word, that he was with
God and that he was God. This is so clear that Jesus
is indeed God. The Jehovah's Witnesses have their
own bible, and they say the Word was with God and
the Word was a God. If this statement is true then
that would imply that there is more than one God.
The Bible is clear that there is only one God. Then
verse fourteen says that the Word was made flesh and
dwelt among us. This is in reference to the humanity and life of the LORD Jesus. This verse by itself
defends the doctrine of the deity of Jesus.

Jesus – Image of the Invisible God

*Who is the image of the invisible God, the
firstborn of every creature: For by him were
all things created, that are in heaven, and that
are in earth, visible and invisible, whether
they be thrones, or dominions, or principalities, or powers: all things were created by
him, and for him.*
(Colossians 1:15-16)

Here scripture says that Jesus is the "image of the invisible God," so when you see Jesus in his earthly ministry you see God in the flesh. This passage also tells us that Jesus is the creator. If he was not God he could not have created. Christ was with God before the creation, during it and after it. Jesus is called "Alpha and Omega, the beginning and the end" in Revelation 1:8, which points out that he was with God at the beginning of time and is God.

Therefore the Jews sought the more to kill him, because he not only had broken the Sabbath, but said also that God was his Father, making himself equal with God (John 5:18). Jesus did not deny that he was equal with God, but acknowledged it. He even accepted worship that was only to be given to God.

Jesus is God

But unto the Son he saith, Thy throne, O God is forever and ever: a scepter of righteousness is the scepter of thy kingdom (Hebrews 1:8). Here we see that God the Father is speaking to the Son, and states *thy throne O God*. The Father declares that his son, Jesus, is also God, and that his throne will last forever.

If ye had known me, ye should have known my Father also: and from henceforth ye know him, and have seen him. Philip saith unto him, Lord, shew us the father and it sufficeth us. Jesus saith unto him, Have I been so long time with you, and yet hast thou not known me, Philip? He that hath seen me hath seen

the Father; and how sayest thou then, Shew
us the Father?
(John 14:7-9)

Philip wanted to see the Father, but Jesus made it very clear if you have seen him you have seen the Father. These verses are very clear and pretty much self-explanatory, but are very important to the Christian Faith.

For in him dwelleth all the fullness of the Godhead bodily (Colossians 2:9). This verse explains itself, that Jesus is totally God.

And without controversy great is the mystery of godliness: God was manifest in the flesh, justified in the Spirit, seen of angels, preached unto the gentiles, believed on in the world, received up into glory (1 Timothy 3:16). Consider these points of discussion in this verse:

- God manifested in the flesh; here we see his incarnation at Bethlehem.
- Seen of angels in his ministry; there was assistance from angels.
- Jesus was preached unto the non-Jews or gentiles.
- Many people throughout his ministry believed on him.
- Jesus was received unto glory at his ascension. Again we clearly see the deity of the LORD Jesus Christ.

For this is good and acceptable in the sight of God our Saviour (1 Timothy 2:3). Here we see that

God is the Savior, and in Matthew 1:21 Jesus is the Savior. Well who is it? It is both because they are one.

Behold a virgin shall be with child, and shall bring forth a son, and they shall call his name Emmanuel, which being interpreted is, God with us (Matthew 1:23). This is a messianic fulfillment of Isaiah 7:14. Jesus is God with us, or in our very presence.

Looking for that blessed hope, and the glorious appearing of the great God and our Saviour Jesus Christ (Titus 2:13). Here we are told to look forward to the return of the Savior, and that he is the great God.

The verses highlighted above clearly state that Jesus is totally God and totally man. Anyone who denies this doctrine is not a believer. We must stand for truth and defend the great doctrines of the faith, and the deity of Jesus is one of them.

Chapter Five:

Jesus Reacts to Temptation

As Christians we face many situations in life, and many temptations come our way. This chapter will show how Jesus reacted when tempted by Satan.

> *There hath no temptation taken you, but such*
> *as is common to man: but God is faithful,*
> *who will not suffer you to be tempted above*
> *that ye are able; but will with the temptation,*
> *also make a way to escape, that ye may be*
> *able to bear it.*
> (1Corinthians 10:13)

You may think when you are tempted that you are the only one going through this situation, but this verse says that all temptations have been around since the beginning of time. Satan and his armies from hell, from the time of the fall to the present, have unleashed all types of temptations on everyone. God will not let you be tempted anymore then you can stand. There will always be a way out and it is through the power of the LORD Jesus Christ.

Jesus Overcomes Temptation

I would like to look at the temptation of Jesus in detail and how he reacted. Let us look at Matthew 4:1-11:

Verse 1: *Then was Jesus led up of the spirit into the wilderness to be tempted of the devil.*

Here we see that Jesus was led by the spirit of God into the wilderness, a place of total serenity and peace, but it did not stay that way. Jesus was to be tempted by the devil. Our LORD was going to come face to face with Satan himself, and the battle would occur. A face to face encounter with Satan is not something we have to deal with. The LORD would face the chief host of hell itself, and would be tempted to sin.

Verse 2: *And when he had fasted forty days and forty nights, he was afterward and hungered.*

Jesus was not only in the wilderness for forty days by himself, but he fasted that time as well. You can only imagine how hungry he was and how weak he was. This was a perfect time for Satan to come into Jesus' midst and tempt him. He was hungry, yet he did not eat; he relied on God's strength.

Verse 3: *And when the tempter came to him, he said, If thou be the Son of God, command that these stones be made bread.*

Considering that Jesus was weak in flesh and hungry, the old devil comes and tells him to make food from the stones. I am sure that Jesus in his humanity was totally tempted to do such a miracle. Satan had to know about his divine power or else he would not have asked him to do such a thing as this. Satan threw food in Jesus' face to get him to sin.

Verse 4: *But he answered and said, It is written, man shall not live by bread alone, but by every word that proceedeth out of the mouth of God.*

Jesus came back at Satan by quoting the Scriptures. When you are tempted to sin and give into Satan's plan and purpose, remember that you have the Sword of the Spirit, which is the Word of God. Notice how Jesus says that man lives by every word that comes from the mouth of God. All scripture is inspired by the Holy Spirit and needs to be believed, obeyed, and taken seriously. The Bible today is under attack by liberals, but it will continue to stand the test of time.

Verses 5-6: *Then the devil taketh him up into the holy city, and setteth him on a pinnacle of the temple. And saith unto him, If thou be the Son of God, cast thyself down: for it is written, He shall give his angels charge concerning thee: and in their hands they shall bear thee up, lest at any time thou dash thy foot against a stone.*

Show me your powers if you are the Son of God. Prove it, for God will surely save you with his angels. Satan now used God's word to tempt Jesus. It amazes me how some people use God's Word, but twist it around to fit what they want to believe. When people look at scripture, they need to keep it in context and compare scripture with scripture. Many preachers today have corrupted God's Word, but they will answer to the LORD for what they have done. Satan knew what he was doing, remember, he is a subtle serpent and he was trying to trick Jesus up.

Verse 7: *Jesus said unto him, It is written again, thou shalt not tempt the Lord thy God.*

Here Jesus again comes right back at Satan by using the scriptures. Always use God's Word when confronting the enemy.

Verses 8-9: *Again the devil taketh him up into an exceeding high mountain, and sheweth him all the kingdoms of the world, and the glory of them. And saith unto him, all these things will I give thee, if thou wilt fall down and worship me.*

Satan took Jesus up to a high place and showed him the kingdoms of the world, offering them to him if he would only worship him. All the kingdoms of the world were not only owned by Jesus, but he created them. Satan in his craftiness thought he could get away with this and have Jesus worship him.

Verse 10: *Then saith Jesus unto him, Get thee hence Satan: for it is written, Thou shalt worship the Lord thy God, and him only shalt thou serve.*

Jesus, for the third time, answered the devil with the Word of God. We are not to worship anyone or anything besides the LORD. We Christians often say that we only worship God and have no idols, but how many times do we put others before the LORD, or sports, or television.

These are idols and other gods that we worship. The LORD wants our total, complete worship, and he deserves it.

Verse 11: *Then the devil leaveth him, and, behold, angels came and ministered unto him.*

Finally the devil left him after three times of trying to get Jesus to sin.

Now we must look at an issue that is debated in theological circles. Though it is not a major doctrine it is food for thought. That is the doctrine of Christ's impeccability versus his peccability. The belief in Christ's peccability holds that since Jesus was a man he could have sinned, but did not. The belief in Christ's impeccability holds that Jesus was God therefore could not sin though he was tempted.

I hold to the doctrine of impeccability, because it shows more the God-man than the man-God view. Remember on the cross, the Father could not even look at Jesus, because he bore the sins of the world on him. If God could not even look at sin, how could he even partake of sin. That is just my view; we can and should agree to disagree on this doctrine.

Let us consider one more verse, 2 Peter 2:9: *The Lord knoweth how to deliver the godly out of temptations.* God knows how to deliver you. When temptations come your way, look to the LORD for strength and in him you will find victory.

Chapter Six:
Jesus and His Precious Promises

There are many promises in the Word of God and they are precious promises. Let us look at ten promises that come straight from the LORD Jesus. When Jesus makes a promise we can be sure he will keep it. We have known people to break promises, and it truly affects us, but Jesus is a promise keeper.

Promise #1: *Therefore take no thought, saying, What shall we eat? or, What shall we drink? or, Wherewithal shall we be clothed? (For after all these things do the Gentiles seek:) for your heavenly Father knoweth that ye have need of all these things. But seek ye first the kingdom of God, and his righteousness; and all these things shall be added unto you.* (Matthew 6:31-33)

This is a promise of provision from God for all those who trust him. Have you ever had a situation where you did not know where the finances would come from to pay the gas or electric bill?

Have you ever lacked food, and did not know what you would eat? The Bible promises that the LORD will not let the righteous be forsaken. God provides for his children. You need not worry about tomorrow for tomorrow will take care of itself. Trust the providing hand of God in every situation in your life. The old hymn states, "Be not dismayed whate'er betide, God will take care of you" This is a promise you can hold onto whenever the tough times come your way and there is a need in your life. God will take care of you.

Promise #2: *Come unto me all ye that labour and are heavy laden, and I will give you rest.* (Matthew 11:28)

Some old sayings declare, "Burdens are lifted at Calvary," and, "Take your burdens to the LORD." When your heart is heavy, and trials come your way, come unto him. When it seems like all hell is breaking loose against you, take your burdens to the LORD. He will help you and also sustain you. Jesus will give you rest for your soul in trying times. Your soul will lie down in the green pastures of rest, and the peace of God will keep you. *Thou wilt keep him in perfect peace, whose mind is stayed on thee: because he trusteth in thee. Trust ye in the LORD forever: for in the LORD JEHOVAH is everlasting strength* (Isaiah 26:3-4). Also in Proverbs 3:5-6: *Trust in the LORD with all thine heart; and lean not unto thine own understanding. In all thy ways acknowledge him, and he shall direct thy paths.*

Trust in the LORD, not on yourselves or anyone else. Leave your burdens at the altar of the LORD.

Promise #3: *And Jesus said unto them, Because of your unbelief: for verily I say unto you, if ye have faith as the grain of a mustard seed, ye shall say unto this mountain, Remove hence to yonder place; and it shall remove; and nothing shall be impossible unto you.* (Matthew 17:20)

This promise is for your growing faith. A mustard seed is the smallest seed, however if you only believe amazing things can happen in your life. You must have faith that God is able to do above that which you ask or think. Do you have things you need in your life and situations you want fixed? Have faith. There are different types of faith, including saving faith, which brings you to Christ, and sustaining faith that keeps you going during tough times believing God through it all.

Hebrews 11 is known as the faith chapter. Verse 1 declares, *Now faith is the substance of things hoped for, the evidence of things not seen.* Faith is believing even when we do not see the results in sight, it is purely trusting Jesus.

Promise #4: *Verily, verily, I say unto you, He that heareth my word, and believeth on him that sent me, hath everlasting life, and shall not come into condemnation; but is passed from death unto life.* (John 5:24)

This, I believe, is one of the greatest promises of Jesus because it is about the eternal security of the believer. This doctrine has been debated for years amongst Bible scholars, and students. I firmly believe a true believer in Jesus cannot lose his salvation. There are many verses to back this up and I would like to look at a couple.

- John 6:35-37: *And Jesus said unto them, I am the bread of life: he that cometh to me shall never hunger; and he that believeth on me shall never thirst. But I said unto you, that ye also have seen me, and believe not. All that the father giveth me shall come to me; and him that cometh to me I will in no wise cast out.* If you receive the LORD as Savior you will never hunger or thirst again. If you could lose your salvation, then you would hunger and thirst again. Jesus also states that when you come to Christ he will not cast you out. Salvation is a complete work of God. You did nothing to earn it and nothing you can do will take it away.

- Hebrews 13:5: *I will never leave thee nor forsake thee.* Jesus will never leave us or separate from us (see Romans 8:35-39). Now this does not give believers an excuse to sin but an encouragement to live for Him.

Since he saved me, he will keep me until that day. Amen and Amen.

Promise #5: *I will not leave you comfortless: I will come to you.* (John 14:18)

This is the promise of the coming of Holy Spirit. Jesus promised that when he ascended he would send another comforter, which is Holy Spirit. The day you became a Christian, you received the Holy Spirit of God, who came into you and sealed you. You do not need to get more of the Spirit, he needs more of you.

Some Christians believe that you have to receive the baptism of the Spirit and speak in tongues. I believe you are baptized in the Holy Spirit at the moment of salvation, and placed into the body of Christ. Daily the Spirit needs to fill you, which is to give him control and live a holy life.

Thank God for the ministry of the Holy Spirit in our lives. Not only does he indwell us, he seals us, baptizes us, and even fills us. He also teaches us all things, and illuminates the Word of God to us.

Promise #6: *But ye shall receive power, after that the Holy Ghost is come upon you: and ye shall be witnesses unto me both in Jerusalem, and in Judea, and in Samaria, and unto the uttermost part of the earth.* (Acts 1:8)

Have you ever had trouble witnessing your faith, or did not know what to say? The Holy Spirit will give you boldness to share your faith with a lost and dying world. Just ask him to help you and to give you boldness to witness. It is important to share your faith. Proverbs 11:30 says, *He that winneth souls is wise.* Nothing is greater in life than to be able to lead a person to the saving knowledge of Jesus Christ.

Promise #7: *These things have I spoken unto you, that my joy might remain in you, and that your joy might be full.* (John 15:11)

Jesus wants to bring joy to the Christian life. Do you feel joyless? Then maybe there is sin in your life, or you are not trusting fully in the

Savior. Knowing Jesus and his salvation should bring joy to every believer.

Promise #8: *And I say also unto thee, That thou art Peter, and upon this rock I will build my church; and the gates of hell shall not prevail against it.* (Matthew 16:18)

The church of Jesus Christ will stand against every vile attack that Satan will throw at it. Throughout the ages many have said that the church will not last and neither would the Bible. But Jesus promised that all of hells fury would not destroy the church of Jesus Christ.

Promise #9: *The thief cometh not, but for to steal, and to kill, and to destroy: I am come that they might have life, and that they might have it more abundantly.* (John 10:10)

Satan attempts to do three things here. The first is to steal, that is to take away your joy. As stated earlier, Satan wants to make you an unhappy Christian. Secondly, he comes to kill your soul and take it to hell with him. If you are not sure of your salvation today, get right with God now and rescue your soul from hell. Third, he comes to destroy your testimony. If you are not living what you profess then you are turning people off to the gospel message. You are accountable to God for how you live once you have accepted Jesus as Savior. The question is how is your testimony? The good news is that Jesus came to give you abundant life in him. A joyous and blessed Christian life.

Promise #10: *He which testifieth these things saith, Surely I come quickly, Amen. Even so, come, Lord Jesus.* (Revelation 22:20)

The last promise in the Bible is recorded by Jesus himself, he is coming back quickly. I am so glad that Jesus will not leave me on this old sinful world, but that he is coming back very soon.

Chapter Seven:

Jesus Promised and Descriptive Return

I love to listen to Southern gospel Music because of all the songs they sing about heaven. They sing a lot about the coming of the LORD. My favorite song is "I'll Fly Away." This chapter will explore two points, the promise of Jesus' return and the description of Jesus return.

Nothing is more exciting than the coming of the LORD and to be ushered home. If you had one desire, what would it be? Would it be having a log cabin in the mountains to get away? Would you like a new car or house? What would be your desire of the LORD?

One Thing I Have Desired

King David shared his desire in Psalm 27:4: *One thing have I desired of the LORD, that will I seek after; that I may dwell in the house of the LORD all the days of my life, to behold the beauty of the LORD, and to enquire in his temple.* David makes it very clear that his desire is to live forever in the house of the LORD and to dwell in glory forever.

Our desire, as stated in Titus 2:13, should be, *Looking for that blessed hope, and the glorious appearing of the great God and our Saviour Jesus Christ.*

Are you looking forward to the return of Jesus? Are you living today as if he were to come? Do you want him to come quickly, like John wrote in Revelation 22:20?

Let Not Your Heart Be Troubled

Let not your heart be troubled: ye believe in God, believe also in me (John 14:1). Are you feeling anxious, troubled, or disturbed? Jesus said to believe in him and to not be troubled or anxious.

Many people today acknowledge God but deny the person of Jesus Christ. The Jews are still waiting for their messiah, which could be a person or even land. However, the promised messiah is in the person of Jesus Christ. In order to have our troubled hearts relieved about the future, people need to trust in Jesus.

In my Father's house are many mansions: if it were not so, I would have told you. I go to prepare a place for you (John 14:2). Jesus began to tell a little about what is in glory, saying that there are mansions in heaven. I have never been in a mansion or even close to one, but up in glory there are mansions for all of us. Jesus is preparing one for you, and me. One day soon, we will have a mansion over the hilltop in that land where we will never grow old. Besides a mansion there are pearly gates, streets of gold, walls of jasper and a clear crystal river. Not only is it beautiful, but there is no more sin, no sorrow and no suffering. What a day that will be, when we reach glory.

And if I go and prepare a place for you, I will come again, and receive you unto myself; that where I am, there ye may be also (John 14:3). This is the promise of Jesus. Remember in the last chapter we looked at the last words of Christ and his promise to come quickly. Here he states if he goes, he will come again! What a promise to the believer. He will not leave us here, but will come and take us home. We will be with him for all eternity, forever and ever. Amen!

Jesus' Promised Return

Now that we have looked at Jesus' promise of return we will turn our focus to the description of his return going through 1 Thessalonians 4:13-18:

Verse 13: *But I would not have you to be ignorant, brethren, concerning them which are asleep, that ye sorrow not, even as others which have no hope.*

The Bible refers to believers who are "asleep." Some Christians believe in the doctrine of soul sleep, in which the soul is in the ground literally sleeping until the resurrection. The word "asleep" in this passage does not mean that at all. The Bible says, *We are confident, I say, and willing rather to be absent from the body, and to be present with the Lord* (2 Corinthians 5:8).

Thus we can see that when a believer dies or falls "asleep," they are automatically in heaven with the LORD. Those who have no hope are asleep as well, but in hell awaiting their final judgment.

Verse 14: *For if we believe that Jesus died and rose again, even so them also which sleep in Jesus will God bring with him.*

This passage reveals that those who believe in the gospel of Jesus will go with him.

Verse 15: *For this we say unto you by the word of the Lord, that we which are alive and remain, unto the coming of the Lord shall not prevent them which are asleep.*

Verse 16: *For the Lord himself shall descend from heaven with a shout, with the voice of the archangel, and with the trump of God: and the dead in Christ shall rise first.*

The Bible describes the LORD descending to come back for his children, which reveals that heaven is way up beyond the blue. A shout of victory and a shout of glory will be heard around the world. Then the voice of an archangel, probably Michael, will be heard from heaven, and then a trumpet will sound (trumpets were used in the Bible for gathering people). This will be the gathering of those who were asleep in Jesus from all over the world.

The dead in Christ, those who passed on who were believers, will be first. Imagine what this will be like; a worldwide grave opening with billions of dead bodies being caught up to meet the LORD in the air where they will receive their new bodies.

Are you tired of your body being over-weight, of wrinkles on your face, or being too tall or too small? Pretty soon you will have a new and glorified body.

Verse 17: *Then we which are alive and remain shall be caught up together with them in the clouds, to meet the Lord in the air: and so shall we ever be with the Lord.*

Those who died in Jesus are caught up to meet the LORD and receive their new bodies. Then we who are alive and are saved in Jesus will disappear in a moment, the twinkling of an eye. This is awesome. In less than a short second all believers will leave this world to go to glory. I can hear CNN now, "Billions disappear world-wide and we do not know what happened!"

There will be worldwide chaos with car accidents from drivers being raptured and planes crashing from pilots being caught up. People will be running in the streets screaming as loved ones disappear. Religious leaders will try to explain what happened. They might say that the evil people have been taken out by God. Maybe some will say that progressive evolution has happened and they just evolved out of existence. Others might say that there has been a mass disappearance caused by unidentified flying objects. Nobody knows what they will say, but that will not stop what has already happened, the rapture of the church.

If you are not sure of your salvation, make sure today, so that you will be caught up in the air, and not left here for the great and terrible day of the LORD.

Verse 18: *Wherefore comfort one another with these words*.

The coming of Jesus to take his church home should bring comfort. Some Christians believe that the church will go through part of the tribulation period, while others believe the church will go through all of the tribulation. I believe that the church will be caught up before the tribulation. How can we take comfort in knowing that we will go through a period of judgment on earth? The judgment is for the world not the church.

Jesus is coming again, whether you believe it or not. I pray that you are prepared for his coming by putting your faith and trust in Jesus alone for your salvation. Again I say come, LORD Jesus, come quickly!

Chapter Eight:
Jesus as Revealed in Revelation

The book of Revelation is one which many preachers stay away from. They say it is too hard to interpret. However, Revelation 1:3 gives a threefold blessing for those who read it, hear it and keep it. There are many great truths in this book such as the coming of the Lord in chapter 4, the seven seal judgments, the seven trumpets, and the seven vials poured out on the earth. It deals with the anti-christ and his false prophet. Revelation also reveals the destruction of political and spiritual Babylon. This chapter will look at five places where Jesus is revealed in this book.

Revelation chapters 2 through 4 record Jesus talking to the seven churches of Asia Minor and how he deals with them. It is important to point out that these were literal local churches that also represent different states of the church in the church age.

Ephesus

First is the church of Ephesus (2:1-7), the church who left its first love. This church was commended for their works, patience, and how they dealt with false teachers. Then they were rebuked for leaving their first love. This happens often in today's church. We do great things for God, follow his word and even share our faith. Then it becomes a ritual and we do it just out of action and come to the point where we leave our first love, Jesus Christ. We must stay in love with him each and every day, asking God to give us fire in our bones to serve him.

Smyrna

Next is the church of Smyrna (2:8-11), the persecuted church. This church was suffering from heavy persecution because of their faith in Jesus. Today around the world there are thousands of Christians who suffer for the name of Jesus. I am not talking about American Christians but those in other countries who are imprisoned for preaching or going to church underground. Many are beaten for the cause of Christ and some are even killed because of faith in Jesus Christ. It is illegal to be a believer in Jesus in most Islamic countries today, and you could be tortured and killed for saying the name of Jesus. We must pray for those who are truly suffering for their faith in Jesus and ask the LORD to give them strength. What is to say that this type of persecution will not happen in America before the LORD returns? Jesus commends this church for their faithfulness even unto death.

Pergamos

Third is the church of Pergamos (2:12-17), the worldly church. Some believers in this church held fast to the LORD'S name and were faithful to him. The majority of this church lived a worldly life, participating in sexual immorality and eating food sacrificed to idols. Today there are many worldly Christians and churches that profess Christ but live like the devil. This type of church stinks in the nostrils of God, and Jesus warned them to repent or face judgment. They did not repent of their ways so God brought judgment their way.

Thyatira

The fourth church is Thyatira (2:18-29), the compromising church. They ate food sacrificed to idols, committed immorality, and mixed the doctrines of Christ with pagan practices for their theology. Again, we see this today. Many churches have mixed the truth of God's Word with practices and theology that are outside of Biblical Christianity. Many churches are new age in philosophy, pagan in practice, or even cultic in theology like the "name it, claim it" folk. Jesus warns of compromising God's Word, or mixing it with a little leaven of error. We need to stay true to old-fashioned, Christ-centered, Bible-based preaching and churches.

Sardis

The fifth church is Sardis (3:1-6), the dead church. They do works and profess the truth, but the truth is not in them. We see this in many of our modern day mainline protestant churches that are completely dead spiritually. They need a fresh work of the Holy Spirit and true Biblical salvation to touch their lives.

Philadelphia

The sixth church is Philadelphia (3:7-13), the faithful church. Philadelphia is the only church that did not receive judgment. Jesus commended them because they kept his Word and stayed true to the scriptures and the doctrine of Christ. They did not compromise, commit immorality, or mix truth and error in their teachings. Jesus also told them that they did not deny his name. They were faithful to the name of Jesus and even when persecuted did not deny who Jesus was. We need churches like this today that are faithful in preaching and practice, churches who will stand for truth, condemn error, and who live holy and separated lives unto the LORD.

Laodicea

The seventh church is Laodicea (3:14-22), the apostate church. This type of church denies the fundamental truths of God's Word. They attack the Bible's authority and even claim it has error. They deny the virgin birth of Jesus and salvation by faith alone.

They attack the trinity and deity of Jesus Christ and is a church in name only. We need to proclaim truth to those who are caught up in this type of social club and present them with the message of hope through Jesus Christ.

Jesus – Faithful Judge

Jesus Christ is a faithful judge who will judge the living and the dead, both those in Christ and those who are not saved. *And behold I come quickly; and my reward is with me, to give every man according as his work shall be* (Revelation 22:12). Here we see that there will be a reward ceremony for those who have trusted Christ. Rewards will be given for how we lived once we have accepted Jesus as Savior.

Revelation 4:4 says, ...*and round about the throne were four and twenty seats: and upon the seats I saw four and twenty elders sitting, clothed in white raiment; and they had on their heads crowns of gold.* The four and twenty elders represent the church in heaven. The gold on their heads are the rewards of their works as believers at the judgment seat of Christ.

The four and twenty elders fall down before him that sat on the throne, and worship him that liveth forever and ever, and cast their crowns before the throne, saying, Thou art worthy, O Lord, to receive glory and honour and power: for thou hast created all things, and for thy pleasure they are and were created. (Revelation 4:10-11)

Believers before the throne will receive their rewards, lay them at the feet of Jesus and then worship him. This will be an awesome experience of true worship when we give our rewards back to Jesus who washed us in his blood.

The other judgment of Christ is for the unsaved, the great white throne judgment:

> *And I saw a great white throne, and him that sat on it, from whose face the earth and the heaven fled away; and there was found no place for them. And I saw the dead small and great, stand before God; and the books were opened: and another book was opened, which is the book of life: and the dead were judged out of those things which were written in the books, according to their works. And the sea gave up the dead which were in it; and death and hell delivered up the dead which were in them: and they were judged every man according to their works. And death and hell were cast into the lake of fire. This is the second death. And whosoever was not found written in the book of life was cast into the lake of fire.*
> (Revelation 20:11-15)

The unsaved souls who are in hell must appear before the throne of God to have their works judged before their final judgment. These people are those whose names are not recorded in the Lamb's Book of Life. The book will be opened to their works on earth and the degree of punishment in the lake of fire that they will receive. Then they will be cast into the lake of fire.

Hell is a place of real fire that will burn the lost souls for all eternity. This is the judgment of all the unsaved who stand before God. Jesus is a just and righteous judge, and will judge the saved and the unsaved.

Jesus – King of Kings

Revelation presents Jesus as the coming King. This will happen at the end of the seven year tribulation period:

And I saw heaven opened, and behold a white horse; and he that sat upon him was called Faithful and True, and in righteousness he doth judge and make war. His eyes were as a flame of fire, and on his head were many crowns; and he had a name written, that no man knew, but he himself, and he was clothed with a vesture dipped in blood: and his name is called the Word of God. And the armies which were in heaven followed him upon white horses, clothed in fine linen, white and clean. And out of his mouth goeth a sharp sword, that with it he should smite the nations: and he shall rule them with a rod of iron: and he treadeth the winepress of the fierceness and wrath of Almighty God. And he hath on his vesture and on his thigh a

*name written, KING OF KINGS, AND LORD
OF LORDS.*
(Revelation 19:11-16)

This passage reveals several things about the
coming King:

He is called Faithful and True. No one is more
faithful and true than Jesus Christ. He is faithful in
every aspect of his character and true to the core.

- His eyes were a flame of fire, which indicates
  judgment is coming.
- His vesture was dipped in blood, which refers to
  his shed blood at Calvary.
- His name is called the Word of God, which is in
  reference to John 1:1 and refers to Jesus as the
  Word.

The passage then mentions armies that follow
Jesus on white horses. This is the church of Jesus
Christ. Remember the church is raptured in
Revelation 4 and then returns from heaven after
the seven years of tribulation on earth. The church,
clothed in fine linen, white and clean, returns with
Christ equipped for the battle of Armageddon. "Fine
linen, white and clean" is a reference to the blood of
Christ making them clean, and the white speaks of
purity. Then we see the judgment, *out of his mouth
goeth a sword which will smite the nations.* All the
armies and nations of the world will be gathered
here to try and defeat Christ in this battle, but when

his word is spoken, the enemy is defeated and mass bloodshed occurs in all the nations of the world.

Jesus – Victorious King

Not only is Jesus the coming King, he is the victorious king as well:

And I saw an angel standing in the sun; and he cried with a loud voice, saying to all the fowls that fly in the midst of heaven, come and gather yourselves together unto the supper of the great God; That ye may eat the flesh of Kings, and the flesh of captains, and the flesh of mighty men, and the flesh of horses, and of them that sit on them, and the flesh of all men, both free and bond, both small and great. And I saw the beast, and the kings of the earth, and their armies, gathered together to make war against him that sat on the horse, and against his army. And the beast was taken, and with him the false prophet that wrought miracles before him, with which he deceived them that had received the mark of the beast, and them that worshipped his image. These both were cast alive into a lake of fire burning with brimstone. And the remnant were slain with the sword of him that sat upon the horse, which sword proceeded out of his mouth: and all the fowls were filled with their flesh.
(Revelation 19:17-21)

Again there are many points to ponder in this passage. First, the birds were to prepare for the *supper of the great God*, which is not a supper you want to attend or even partake in. This is a bloody and fleshy feast upon the bodies of dead people who lost their war with Christ. When Christ spoke the armies were defeated, and all the bodies of kings and captains who were killed were eaten. The horses and those who rode on them were killed. Then the fowls came down and had a fleshy feast on their bodies.

Then the beast and false prophet who deceived the masses, those that took the mark, are cast into the lake of fire. The mark of the beast is the number six hundred and sixty six and is placed on the hand or forehead of those who received it. During the tribulation there will come a time when people will not be able to buy or sell unless they have received the mark. However, when the mark is received, those who are marked are damned to hell. Those who refuse the mark and accept Christ during the tribulation period might have to give their lives up for the LORD.

I would rather accept Christ today than live in the tribulation and maybe face death for accepting Christ then. Today is the day of salvation, not tomorrow.

Finally, Jesus will reign as King. He will come back to earth with his saints to reign and rule for one thousand years, which is the millennial reign of Christ. This Kingdom will only include believers, the saints of old and tribulation saints, and Jesus will be their King. In this kingdom there will be no more wars:

And he shall judge among many people, and rebuke strong nations afar off; and they shall beat their swords into plowshares, and their pears into pruninghooks: nation shall not lift up a sword against nation, neither shall they learn war anymore.
(Micah 4:3)

Thus saith the LORD; I am returned unto Zion, and will dwell in the midst of Jerusalem: and Jerusalem shall be called a city of truth; and the mountain of the LORD of hosts the holy mountain. Jerusalem will be political and spiritual hub in the millennial Kingdom, and Jesus will be the center of worship.
(Zechariah 8:3)

The wolf also shall dwell with the lamb, and the leopard shall lie down with the kid; and the calf and the young lion, and the fatling together; and a little child shall lead them. And the cow and the bear shall feed down together: and the lion shall eat straw like the ox. And the sucking child shall play on the hole of the asp, and the weaned child shall put his hand on the cockatrice den. They shall not hurt or destroy in all my holy mountain:

*for the earth shall be full of knowledge of the
LORD, as the waters cover the sea.*
(Isaiah 11:6-9)

There will be peace among all animals like there
was in the garden and they will not hunt or eat flesh.
Children will play around the dens of deadly snakes
and will not get bitten. This will be a Kingdom of
universal peace and prosperity. The LORD Jesus
will reign with the saints, and the feasts of Israel
will be restored.

I cannot wait to be a part this kingdom . Will you
join me there?

Chapter Nine:
Jesus and His Glorious Gospel

Everyone likes to hear good news instead of bad news. The gospel of Jesus Christ is exactly that, so let us look at seven points:

Point #1: *MOREOVER, brethren, I declare unto you the gospel which I preached unto you, which also ye have received, and wherein ye stand: By which also ye are saved, if ye keep in memory what I have preached unto you, unless ye have believed in vain. For I delivered unto you first of all that which I also received, how that Christ died for our sins according to the scriptures: And that he was buried, and that he rose again the third day according to the scriptures.* (1 Corinthians 15:1-4)

The message of the gospel is in three parts. First, the death of Christ. Notice that it says *according to the scriptures*. This is in reference to Isaiah 53, Psalm 22 and other passages that talk about the death of messiah. The death of Jesus was brutal and gruesome; he was beaten, spat upon, and whipped with a cat-of-nine-tails. The beating was so severe that when they struck him with the cat-of-nine-tails, his intestines literally came out. The Roman soldiers crushed thorns into his skull, and nails were driven into his hands and feet. This torture unto death caused excruciating pain and mass bleeding of the body and the brain.

Jesus did not simply faint on the cross as some liberal preachers believe. He literally died a cruel death. His burial is also referenced in the scriptures, declaring that he was placed in a new tomb with a huge stone rolled in front of it:

Now the next day, that followed the day of preparation, the chief priests, and Pharisees came together unto Pilate, Saying Sir we remember that that deceiver said, while he was yet alive, after three days I will rise again. Command therefore that the sepulcher be made sure until the third day, lest his disciples come by night, and steal him away, and say unto the people, He is risen from the dead: so the last error shall be worse than the first. Pilate said unto them, Ye have a watch: go your way, make it as safe as you can. So they went, and made the sepulcher sure, sealing the stone, and setting a watch.
(Matthew 27:62-66)

This tomb was not a usual burial plot. It had an extremely large stone in front and it was sealed shut. Guards were posted in front to watch for those sneaky disciples who might try to roll the stone away. Why would they even think about it since after Christ's death they became skeptics of unbelief? Would they consider risking their lives for something they doubted? I do not think so.

Jesus literally died on Calvary's cross. His body was placed in a well-known tomb that was sealed with a large stone with guards watching it day and night. So there is no way his body could get out, right? Not so, the third part of the gospel is victory, and Jesus has risen from the dead.

On that third day, two women named Mary came to Jesus' grave site and found that the stone had been rolled away.

And the angel answered and said unto the woman, fear not ye: for I know that ye seek Jesus: which was crucified. He is not here: for he is risen as he said, Come see the place where the Lord lay.
(Matthew 28:5-6)

Jesus was not there, he was risen from the dead. Satan could not keep him down. Thanks be to God who gives us the victory through our LORD Jesus Christ. The gospel message is good news of the death, burial, and resurrection of Jesus Christ.

Point #2: *For I am not ashamed of the gospel of Christ: for it is the power of God unto salvation to every one that believeth; to the Jew first, and also to the Greek*. (Romans 1:16)

The second point is the power of the gospel. The gospel of Jesus has so much power it can save a soul from a devils hell, there is nothing else this side of heaven that can do that. Paul also states that he is not ashamed of the gospel of Jesus Christ.

Do you get embarrassed about your faith, or ashamed to share it because people might mock you? Tell this message to everyone you know. Shout from the mountain tops, from the pulpits, and all the way to Washington D.C., that Jesus is risen indeed!

Point #3: *But though we, or an angel from heaven, preach any other gospel unto you than that which we have preached unto you, let him be accursed*. (Galatians 1:8)

The third point is the preaching of another gospel. If someone preaches a message to you that is contrary to the message of Christ's gospel, have nothing to do with them. There will be false preachers in the last days (Matthew 24:11). Scripture declares that if an angel preaches another message, let him be accursed. The cult of Mormonism was started by a message from an angel, so be careful of the cults out there and stay true to the gospel message.

Point #4: *If ye continue in the faith grounded and settled, and be not moved away from the hope of the gospel, which ye have heard, and* *which was preached to every creature which is under heaven; whereof I Paul am made a minister.* (Colossians 1:23)

The fourth point is the hope of the gospel which gives hope to a dark and dying world. This world has no hope except for the gospel of Jesus Christ. This word hope literally means a guarantee and a promise.

Point #5: *And if Christ be not risen, then is our preaching vain, and your faith is also vain. Yea, and we are found false witnesses of God; because we have testified of God that he raised up Christ: whom he raised not up, if so be that the dead rise not . . . Then they also which are fallen asleep in Christ are perished. If in this life only we have hope in Christ, we are of all men most miserable.* (1 Corinthians 15:14-15, 18-19)

The fifth point is the importance of the gospel. This message of the gospel is so important that if Christ was still dead then our preaching and faith would be in vain. If Jesus did not rise again, Bibles could be discarded, churches closed and witnessing ceased because it would be a false witness of something that did not really happen. As for those who believed in Jesus and died, there would be no hope and they would perish to a devils hell. As professing believers, if Christ is not alive, then we are most miserable. Therefore, everything rises and falls on the gospel message.

Point #6: *So when this corruptible, shall have put on incorruption, and this mortal shall have put on immortality, then shall be brought to pass* *the saying that is written, Death is swallowed up in victory. O death, where is thy sting? O grave, where is thy victory? The sting of death is sin; and the strength of sin is the law. But thanks be to God, which giveth us the victory through our Lord Jesus Christ.* (1 Corinthians 15:54-57)

The sixth point is the results of the gospel, a new body. There is no spiritual death for believers, we have victory. Victory in Jesus, our savior forever!

Point #7: *Therefore, my beloved brethren, be ye stedfast, unmoveable, always abounding in the work of the Lord, forasmuch as ye know that your labour is not in vain in the Lord.* (1 Corinthians 15:58)

The seventh point is response to the gospel. How do you respond to the life-changing message of the gospel of Jesus? Are you steadfast and unmovable, because nothing should move you as you are standing on the Rock of Ages. Are you serving the LORD in your church or community? If not, then why? Remember whatever you do for Jesus is never in vain, so go out and serve him wherever he leads you.

The gospel of Jesus Christ is the greatest message we have. It changes lives forever and gives hope to all. Remember the first two letters in gospel are "go," so go preach it to every person and watch God work in great ways.

Chapter Ten:
Jesus' Invitation to All

Throughout this book the life, ministry and person of Jesus Christ have been examined. With all that said and done I would like to give you an invitation that will change your life. The greatest decision you can ever make is to receive Jesus Christ as LORD and savior. Outlined below are seven passages of scripture that deal with salvation.

Jesus stands at the door: *Behold, I stand at the door, and knock: if any man hear my voice, and open the door, I will come into him, and will sup with him, and he with me.* (Revelation 3:20)

Jesus is presently standing at the door of your heart and knocking to come in. He will not force himself on you, but will leave the decision up to you to let him in your life. The Holy Spirit will convict you of sin and your need for the savior. What you do with that decision will determine your eternal destination.

Life eternal: *And this is life eternal, that they might know thee the only true God, and Jesus Christ, whom thou hast sent.* (John 17:3)

Today you can know God on a personal level through Jesus Christ. You can know for sure that you are heaven-bound and have a relationship with the God of the universe through Jesus Christ.

Confess with your mouth: *That if thou shalt confess with thy mouth the Lord Jesus, and shalt believe in thine heart that God hath raised him from the dead, thou shalt be saved. For with the heart man believeth unto righteousness; and with the mouth confession is made unto salvation.* (Romans 10:9-10)

When you confess with your mouth and believe with all your heart the gospel message of Jesus Christ, you will be saved. It is not a work-oriented message, but a message of faith in Jesus Christ.

Call upon the name of the Lord: *For whosoever shall call upon the name of the Lord shall be saved.* (Romans 10:13)

This is an invitation to everyone, man, woman, boy and girl; everyone can come to Jesus today. The message of Christ is for whosoever will call upon him. If you repent of your sins, and give your heart to Jesus you will be saved.

Sons of God: *But as many as received him, to them gave he power to become the sons of God, even to them that believe on his name.* (John 1:12)

To become a son and daughter of God, receive Jesus as savior today. If someone offered you a one-hundred dollar bill, and you would have to take it for it to become yours. If you open your hands and receive it then it is yours to have and keep. The same is true of salvation. You must receive it before you can call it yours. Receive Jesus as savior today, before it is too late. Today is the day of salvation.

Jesus is the way, the truth and the life: *Jesus saith unto him, I am the way, the truth, and the life: no man cometh unto the Father, but by me*. (John 14:6)

Jesus is the only way to God. Today many churches preach that Jesus is a way, not the way. Any road outside of Jesus Christ leads to hell. Jesus is also the truth and in him there is no sin or error. Jesus takes people who are spiritually dead and brings them to life in him.

God so loved the world: *For God so loved the world, that he gave his only begotten Son, that whosoever believeth in him should not perish, but have everlasting life. For God sent not his Son into the world to condemn the world; but that the world through him might be saved*. (John 3:16-17)

The good news today is that God loves you regardless of your sin. Because of his love for you, he gave his Son to die on Calvary's cross. What greater love is there than a man who would lay down his life for his brother? If you believe in Jesus and trust him as savior, you will not perish or go to hell, but will go to heaven when the LORD calls you home.

Have you personally received Jesus as your Savior? If not, I would like to share a prayer with you that you can pray to receive him. It is not the words that save you, but the cry of your heart. If you pray this simple prayer in faith and believe what you are saying, you will be saved.

Dear LORD, I acknowledge that I am a sinner. I believe that Jesus died on the cross for my sins, and rose again on the third day. I repent of my sins. By faith, I receive the LORD Jesus as my personal savior. You promised to save me and I believe you, because you are God and cannot lie. I believe right now that the LORD Jesus is my savior, and that all of my sins are forgiven through his precious blood. I thank you for saving me. In Jesus' name. Amen.

If you just prayed that prayer and truly meant it, you are now a saved believer in Jesus Christ. I want to encourage you to read your Bible daily, starting in the book of John. Then find a Bible-believing church and begin attending on a regular basis.

May God bless each and every person reading this book. If you read this book may your relationship with Jesus be stronger and sweeter each and every day.

About the Author

Rev. Daren Drzymala is a Bible-believing Baptist minister who resides in Buffalo, NY. He graduated from the late Dr. Jerry Falwell's, Liberty University. He presently fills the pulpit for churches in the Buffalo area. He has a strong desire to see people everywhere come to a personal relationship with Jesus Christ and to become grounded in the Word of God.

To contact Rev. Drzymala email him at
Baptistpreacher7@hotmail.com
and Baptistpreacher7@juno.com

CPSIA information can be obtained
at www.ICGtesting.com
Printed in the USA
FFHW021938020120
57464858-62904FF